T0206638

LOVE WILL BURST INTO A THOUSAND SHAPES

LOVE WILL BURST INTO
A THOUSAND SHAPES

JANE EATON HAMILTON

CAITLIN PRESS

Copyright © 2014 Jane Eaton Hamilton
01 02 03 04 05 18 17 16 15 14
All poems are fictional and are not based on nor intended to make comments on actual events.

All rights reserved. No part of this publication may be reproduced, stored in a retrieval system or transmitted, in any form or by any means, without prior permission of the publisher or, in the case of photocopying or other reprographic copying, a licence from Access Copyright, the Canadian Copyright Licensing Agency, www.accesscopyright.ca, 1-800-893-5777, info@accesscopyright.ca.

Caitlin Press Inc.
8100 Alderwood Road,
Halfmoon Bay, BC V0N 1Y1
www.caitlin-press.com

Edited by Patricia Young
Text design by Holly Vestad
Cover design by Vici Johnstone
Cover art by Catrin Welz-Stein
Printed in Canada

Caitlin Press Inc. acknowledges financial support from the Government of Canada through the Canada Book Fund and the Canada Council for the Arts, and from the Province of British Columbia through the British Columbia Arts Council and the Book Publisher's Tax Credit.

Canada Council   Conseil des Arts
for the Arts   du Canada

BRITISH COLUMBIA
ARTS COUNCIL

Library and Archives Canada Cataloguing in Publication
Hamilton, Jane Eaton, author
Love will burst into a thousand shapes / Jane Eaton Hamilton.
Poems.
ISBN 978-1-927575-57-4 (pbk.)
I. Title.

PS8565.A553L68 2014   C811'.54   C2014-904123-3

OTHER BOOKS BY JANE EATON HAMILTON

Body Rain (Brick Books, 1991)
"Jane Eaton Hamilton is not a poet content to whisper in your ear or take you on slow walks through pretty fields. She sits you down in her hardest chair, litters tacks on the floor about your naked feet, and holds you there petrified but alert as she speaks the body's news." —LEON ROOKE

July Nights (Douglas & McIntyre, 1992)
"These are die-hard stories full of perilous honesty. I love Hamilton's creatures: they have flesh and blood and bones. They tell the truth even when it's as surprising as graffiti— tender-hearted and furious and right off the wall." —LINDA SPALDING

Steam-Cleaning Love (Brick Books, 1993)
"Reading [these poems] is like reading other people's letters until, by the transforming magic good poems have, you discover they are all for you." —JANE RULE

Going Santa Fe (League of Canadian Poets, 1997)
"Going Santa Fe is extraorinarilee accomplished n sew honest evree world adds n multiples nevr misses a beet unbelievable tendr strong n totalee reel sew liberating a book yu embrace with yr mind n yr heart." —BILL BISSETT

Hunger (Oberon Press, 2002)
"Jane Eaton Hamilton is a superb writer. Those who do not know this should read the book and judge for themselves." —JOY KOGAWA

"These stories will grab you by the throat and not let you go. Highly original, gripping, sharp and deeply moving, they deserve the prizes they have won, and those to come." —EMMA DONOGUE

"Jane Eaton Hamilton is a fine and accomplished writer." —CAROL SHIELDS

This book is in memory of Candis Graham.

TABLE *of* CONTENTS

THIS NEW COUNTRY

HANDS

TREMBLEMENT DE TERRE

Tremblement de Terre: Suzanne Valadon

Fifteen, la fille blanche, she rose, swung high
floated under big top
acrobat on trapeze
then tumbled
past elephants, monkeys in top hats, clowns
the jiggering tiger

She broke in the circus ring
paintbrush between teeth
corsage of carrots pinned to her chest
simple, abstract
distorted and pure
(a goatish one)
le fauve rouge

rose again, an artist

A Terrible Lucidity, 1890: Vincent Van Gogh

My nephew ill, Theo collapsing
I careen around bucking fields
One is one's own horse, harrowing; one is one's own love for God
but so what?
I can't save anybody; I funnel them down
my ineptitude
I am a waste
Theo knows it; his hope, like my own, gone
And why not?
Evening shutters the day
clouds collapse in drowned sorrow
the stars drop halos
I cannot capture
my gratitude

Later, after the drink
when the whore in her swirling skirt has
swished down cobblestones
I think of Paul
who took my ear and claimed he'd never
bent me over the bug-ridden mattress

In dreams I comprehend absolution

Everyone has something to say about my disgrace
(*Give me money*)
the canvases stacked like so many francs I should have spent
on rent or soup

God laughs—I hear him in the fields
choirmaster of the sublime
His voice on a wave of wind
Believe this, will you?
Everyone says voices are my disease
but they are wrong

Vincent, be still, they say, but
I have tried inertia
Nothing was possible
in the narrow asylum bed
with the whey-faced sheets
I was absent and clean, but—

Doesn't anyone understand tilting at windmills?

In the morning
it is all I can do to push brush into pigment
just once
a single redemptive time is all I ask

I am here, I am here!
Crows slice clouds
wheat sheaves caterwaul
I paint them as they toss
into bruised shadows

I am only ruined hands
What I have shaped
is not what I meant

Stop! stop!

Then, for a moment
perfection, a second
of clarity
Light translated

and then
a second later, perfection
denied

The Lucite Box: Edward Degas

A flower of precocious depravity.
—CRITICS RESPONDING TO *LA PETITE DANSEUSE DE QUATORZE ANS*, A DEGAS
SCULPTURE, AT THE SIXTH IMPRESSIONIST EXHIBITION OF 1881, PARIS, FRANCE

I circle the box
at Musée d'Orsay
as Degas must have circled the child
How to hammer this
million-dollar baby loose?
She was *marked by the hateful promise of every vice*
boxed like a gift

A sledge on the Lucite, surely
a heavy saw?

Bronzed legs (their hatch marks)
open fourth
slippers, braid, hair ribbon
bustier, worn cotton tutu
Forbearing chin
Chest, a child's, extended

In the work of holding the pose
while Degas fiddled with armature
wire and paintbrushes
did she find ecstatic patience?

Little rat, gritty guttersnipe
muscles strained
tendons screamed

If I freed her, where would she go
set loose into 2014, roaming
the d'Orsay
for crumbs?

I circle her
and imagine him, bearded, waistcoated
touching pencil
paintbrush

Was it love
(brute, anguished
exhausted)?

Was it rape, this
sponsored patronage?
Men in the foyer de la danse
tipped top hats, bartered opera tickets
for girls

Degas, the voyeur losing his sight
rented Marie by the hour
Now working in sculpture
fat fingers sinking deep into
hot wax

Marie, foot pushed toward us
as if lowered from a gentleman's lap

ODALISQUE AT NICE: MATISSE

Henriette
you slip over my paintbrush
like Morocco, like turpentine
the ugliness of blood on a monthly Monday
I despise that which heats me
The lines of my pen disgust me

Your mouth is a tube of colour
Up and down, down and up, it moves
as lips fold over teeth

You ought to be en pointe
You ought to be at the piano
Not here, being ruined by an old man
my hungers and horrible hands

Petals fall
scatter pointlessly behind the green divan
hours of wasted contemplation

I want to absolve myself, Henriette
Wake up
I crave the cleanliness of your seduction
not this black hue of rape
as paint dries

Love Will Burst into a Thousand Shapes[1]: Frida Kahlo

The first time I married Diego
he could not lift the paintbrush
from my womb
I bled cadmium from interior spaces
yawning with pubic hair, seeds
cactus roots
cavernous with absence
feeding myself with the milk of Solanaceae
Demeter's teats
spitting out sugary skeletons
instead of babies
slipping toward parthenogenesis

After I married Diego a second time
he wound necklaces of thorns around my throat
I bled alizarin crimson from soft flesh
feeding myself dead birds
Other women crowded around
masticating and cheering, but they were nothing
even my sister was nothing
(was I? Was I nothing? With my lovers?)

Diego grabbed the sky
through the cavern in my chest
his arm a straight unbearable pole
and told me that was all the love
he had

---

1   Frida Kahlo, note to Diego Rivera

Fair is fair; I didn't have a heart anymore
just something swollen
a girl's red castle of pain
wetly beating on sand

WOMAN WITH A MANGO, BY GAUGUIN: ETTA CONE[2]

Gertrude you are a Gertrude are a Gertrude
no one in Baltimore is a Gertrude anymore
If you can't say anything nice about anyone
come sit next to me
you said
and I did
under *Mother and Child* come sitting
in Baltimore in Paris in Baltimore
no one is a Gertrude is a Gertrude enough

There were the two of us, you said, we were not sisters
We were not large not then we were not rich
we were not so different one from the other one
an eye was an eye was an eye, gazing

A woman would smell
a woman would hold out her smell and smell and petals
would drop from *Large Reclining Nude*
white petals cool and fragrant and soft
and dropping and dropping and dropping down
Three Lives my fingers sore my wrists aching typing
Come sit next to me you said
and I did sit I did sit I sat and sat and after I sat I sat and sat

I typed until the "G" key stuck
Three lives, yours, Claribel's, mine
I was sitting and sitting under
Woman with a Mango under *Blue Nude*

---

2   With reference to *Three Lives*, *Stanzas in Meditation* (VII) and *Sacred   Emily*, by
Gertrude Stein.

22

I was sitting with textiles draped over me
hoping their weight
but they are not you, because you have—
Alice? Alice? Alice?

Is an Alice?
Gertrude you undertake to overthrow my undertaking
You say my desiccated loneliness is
across the ocean in Baltimore and you pull Alice onto
your lap on the large brown broken armchair
where you sat with me
while Pablo's portrait strains above
You sit, running Alice's hair through your hands
her hair through your fingers
Your fingers in my hair unpinning tangling
your lips against my neck
There is no there there now
anymore
there is Henri there is Vincent there is Paul and Paul there is Gustave
my neck a neck is a neck with a rose
that died and petals like brown rain
I like what is, you said
I like what is mine I like it

REMARKABLE NUDE 3: THE CELLIST

It began
as adolescent things often begin
with acidulation
she was curdled and rancid, into
deathrock, post-punk, dark e/missions
until the feeling of the cello
between her legs
four strings in perfect fifths
pizzicato, spiccato, staccato
sul ponticello, downbow, upbow
cello-punk from Absent Minds
the wonderfulness of her spread-legged
crotch-open pose, her clit a small pluckable instrument
On her visible breast, ruby of one blood drop
the bareness of knees, skin stretched blanched over bone
ethereal skin pallorous, Manic Panic dreamtones
Every midnight nocturnal music was benison
against darkness
f-hole, tail spike
peg box, scroll, fingerboard
and her short segmented fingers
black nails
her bow dragging and leaping
until dawn took it doggy-style
over the horizon
Along the cellist's ribs, scars from cutting
a hundred thickened quarter notes

OUR TERRIBLE GOOD LUCK

War Photograph

He is perfect, this boy of say seven
hands behind his head, a universal
fat cat—
but
his eyes tell of anything but satiety
assume horror
around the corner (the day, the village, the future)
his back arches, ribs push out
Skin holds
but he knows it could rip
under the slap of a machete

It's impossible to say why he preens
what impulse moves his muscles but
the stump of his amputated leg
lifts in dancers' delight

Hurricane Sandy, NYC, 2012

*The children's part-time nanny is accused of stabbing the children to
death while their mother and 3-year-old sister were a few blocks away at
a swimming lesson.*

—Wikipedia

All day, sea breaches
heaving into subways onto runways into homes
All day rain rides winds
to batter windows
the city dark as pulse

Days earlier, what were the costumes?
Let's imagine: *Where the Wild Things Are* for him
tossed over the crib
and for her, the lobster from Pottery Barn
on hobnail bedspread

The mother blew bubbles
splashing, laughing
ensuring water safety in a world
where nothing is certain
(though everything is prayed for)

In the tub at home
animal cracker towels, berry bubbly bath
Outside the storm brewing
blackening over sea, lashing, and we finally knew:
Those who love can't merge

CHRISTMAS TREE IN JANUARY

for Elizabeth Barbeau

In the long, subdued dusk that is winter
you watch the forbearance of the crow
dripping under the eave; you listen to the coyote's
yipping as she moves skinny-ribbed
and high-legged below your trampoline
burrowing for mice through leaf-fall

It is the absence of light—
the day grown black by four, plummeting
into purples—
this makes you sigh
weather rattling the doorknob
even the shadows have shadows
You go upstairs early; sleep uneasily

turning like a bulb under soil
its onion-skin coat
You rise, stand in the doorway
to your son's room
He coils, a new spring fern
dreaming red engines

There are things you would give this child
his thin snowy throat, his body elongating—
assurances, insurance (your life)
There are things you would tell him about his
fragile beginning and how since then, every day
spins from zero into perfection

Even in January, even now
even as you pad downstairs
to plug in the tree, there is something you would tell him
about banishing darkness and cold
about a thousand steady lights—
Each alone is just solace, but together they make morning

MILKTINI

I) *The Broom*

is a pole with attached bristles
The broom can stand in a closet and be seen by no one
The broom comes alive only in hands:

a woman's hands
ordinary, tremoring
sweeping mouse nests and spiderwebs across the kitchen tile
toward the living-room carpet
under the underlay they lump like live things

The problem of cash
The problem of the vomiting child
The problem of varicose veins
The problem of the car's bald tires
The problem of the husband's fist

At the intersection of 14th and Quebec
a broom—turquoise, plastic, short black bristles
has been struck, its pole twisted and warped,
the head dethroned

II) *The Sponge*

is not what the woman calls for when
her head splits, but it is all the boy thinks
to grab from the silver belly of the sink
and what he holds to her blood-clotted hair

It is the same sponge swiped the night before
across pork gravy

III) *The Bucket*

is worn by the boy when he wants to
shut out fighting
Is yellow. Has a
compartment to wring out the mop
When the boy wears the bucket he believes
he is invisible, an action hero
who can zip through the battle zone
as invisible as his mother
who is known to be clumsy
who calls in sick on average four days every month

IV) *The Vacuum*

was originally her mother's vacuum
Is so old it has a fabric electrical cord
a two-pronged plug

The bags fill up like paper pregnancies
to be discarded
She would like a wet-dry vac

The vacuum makes an unholy roar. Sounds like aircraft

V) *The Mop*

also combats dirt
the kind that adheres

the way a bruise adheres
When dinner is flung from the table
a broom will take care of the mess
(Caesar salad, green beans, rice, salmon)
but anything wet
blood in particular
leaves a sticky film

The mop is a fright wig
a Medusa head

VI) *The Toilet Bowl Cleanser*

Pine-Sol. The boy adds it to water
where it turns to milk
While his mother serves ice cream
he passes it to his father
Milktini, Dad! Drink your milktini!

After the Basketball Game the Girl Attends the Clinic Because She Missed Two Periods

Do you use birth control? the doctor asks
Yes, she says, *I'm on the pill*
How do you take it? the doctor asks
*I swallow one after each time we
do it,* the girl says

VIRGIN #479
(OF 10.113 INSURED)

There are things you can do [to keep your purity], like layering,
accessorizing ...

—RACHEL LEE CARTER

If I conceive God's child my father will get $500,000
My father instructs me to pray for this fortune
he could open a second restaurant
a walk-in fridge

But the truth is that when
I am on my knees I do not pray for
God in my womb

There is a boy at school
who has a laugh like a drum
who is good at geography and Spanish

I am my father's biggest asset, he says
my purity his command

I drink water from the bottom rim of the cup
I swallow twenty Rolaids
my friend says write *I am a whore* on a piece of paper, crumple it
throw it out the window
I squirt Coca-Cola up myself

When I kneel before the priest at the altar
all I ask for is blood

Our Terrible Good Luck

The spot inside the sick boy's brain
burrowed there pale as a tuber
stubborn and engorged. His hair lifted
from his scalp like angel fuzz; his eyes
gleamed and struck us

We watched him
teeter to the lip of the nest, his skin traced blue with veins
Premature fledgling, we thought, and gathered our children closer,
under shivering arms. The sick boy wanted Christmas
cards and he got thousands, maybe millions
a Guinness record, cards enough
to fill warehouses, from everywhere

There was his father, his mother
his sister and brother, the cards
and there was his brain cancer
spreading like a bleach spot
toward September and death

We almost
knew something dangerous that glowed
We almost saw reflections of silver in the mirror
But then we only saw ourselves, lustrous
as poster paints, our terrible good luck

The Drowning

In the month before they find your son's body
downstream, you wake imagining
his fist clutching the spent elastic
of his pyjama bottoms, the pair with sailboats riding them
He's swimming past your room toward milk and Cheerios
his cowlick alive on his small head, swimming
toward cartoons and baseballs, toward his skateboard
paddling his feet like flippers. You're surprised
by how light he is, how his lips shimmer like water
how his eyes glow green as algae
He amazes you again and again, how he breathes
through water. Every morning you almost drown
fighting the undertow, the wild summer runoff
coughing into air exhausted, but your son is happy
He's learning the language of gills and fins
of minnows and fry. That's what he says
when you try to pull him to safety; he says he's a stuntman
riding the waterfall down its awful lengths
to the log jam at the bottom pool
He's cool to the touch; his beauty has you by the throat
He's translucent, you can see his heart under
his young boy's ribs, beating
as it once beat under the stretched skin of your belly
blue as airlessness, primed for the vertical dive

THE TWINS

We watched TV, my daughter and I
  sitting forward on the couch
our legs and arms aligned, pressing
  as if we could get a hint
of what it was like to be conjoined

Once we had shared a body, of course
  but that was twelve years ago
Look, Mom! Meghann said. *Only two*
  legs! those two words repeating
(two legs, two legs) as the girls on the screen

toddled on their two legs, as their
  two legs whistled them sweet down
a playground slide. Top-heavy, joined hip
  to shoulder, each had a spine
a heart and lungs, but they shared kidneys

intestines, liver, blood and also
  their red bud of sex. To part
them was to part something none of us
  could understand. If they were
sweaters, yanks of wool would unravel them

Then they could be knit again
  separate but whole
Their mother brought Cabbage Patch dolls to
  the hospital, Velcroed tight
and showed them how it would be, apart

The rip was loud
Won't they miss each other? asked
Meghann, and I didn't know how to
  say I missed her even when
she slipped out of me

I didn't know how to say their pain
  would be vaster than the folds
of any mother's love
  I nodded, kissed her and
pulled her close

Four days later, one twin died, her own
  heart not healthy, not sound, not good
Under my arms, I could feel
  Meghann's beating strong
beating clear

On TV, the surviving twin craned left
  eyes huge
bewildered, thrust
  into a too-large silence
Meghann clutched me
  and cried

Half a Baby

I'd been there
to photograph the woman's belly, that tiny unyeasted loaf
that Lilliputian bump, that craving convexity that yearned toward
life but could not manage
and the baby's father, who tucked his hand atop
the still-beating second heart of his wife
this firstborn son to this couple
who had believed they were charmed

I was also there when the night turned soft
a hush, only the three of us at 4 a.m., and something
tangible in the air, brushing our skins
tender as feathers whispering our arms, our necks

Just—don't
Don't tell me how macabre
it was with my camera, its heavy clacking
We were there, three of us, then four
five briefly, then four, then three
and the night was more astonishing than
the love I feel for my daughters
the night was more blistering than divorce
and we loved each other

He was only twenty weeks, halfway to whole, half a baby
half a son, halfway, pushing down and out
and when his miniature head finally crowned
showing a black whorl of hair
time shuddered a little before dripping from the clock
The child slid through his mother's labouring cervix

no bigger than dust
He sank through her vagina gasping toward air
and parentage, slipping through hot bleed
A nurse caught him, small in her palm
wrapped him in a green receiving blanket
his lips as round as a cherry as he started to breathe
and breathed

She passed him to his mother's breasts and left us
His blue birth eyes jittered and opened
the lashes wet-clumped and his mother said
He has your ears
and her husband said *He has your lips*
He was covered in a web of blue veins
extra skin he never filled, protuberant bones
a dangling cord, vernix, meconium

It felt like silver rain
The parents named him Christopher Jerome, speaking his name
Soon he convulsed, shivered an undersized death rattle, and stopped
And stopped

I talked to him, to them
There we are, there we go, brave boy
sweet boy, and in this rare and grieving moment
I tried to speak his silence
I'm just going to lift, I told him, and
photographed his hand, the size of a quarter, as if clasping
first his mother's, then his father's fingers
Now, ChristopherJerome, I said, I said again, *there now*
His mother touched her sore hurting lips to his forehead

Don't—
Don't speak to me
Just don't

WENDY M

Every day after school you walked home beside me
past Mr. Smith's fields where the corn rippled high
along our driveway below the maples and oaks
around our farmhouse where I ate, slept, bathed
past the rope swing, the tack house, the chipmunks, the squirrels
past my pet hawk in his aviary
past the mouse-gnawed feed bins into the barn
Shetlands pushed velvet snouts toward us
wanting sugar cubes or apples
You held my hand, surging us forward until
I tugged you back

Hay motes floated through beams of light
We could smell ammonia, straw, shit
we could even smell each other
You knew what you yearned toward—
a horse, just a horse, a horse
Your uncombed hair flew in static
You whispered in my ear
Palomino or pinto
I wanted to wear pants to school
to be a boy, to kiss you
I wanted my brother to pull us in the sulky
I didn't want a horse, another horse

The mare whickered, swatted her tail
whips across skin (we knew)
The farrier yanked nails from her shoe
long, thick, black, tugging free
clattering to the floor

He hasped across hoof until a half moon
fell to the barn floor
The dog darted in, raced away with it
while the farrier shaped a molten shoe on the forge
Pheasants chucked along roof beams

Heat reddened our faces
I held your palm up; lines runneled with dirt
I pricked your palm with a pin; you gasped but didn't run
We watched a blood bead shining
a jewel, a ruby ring
I pricked my palm next
happy with pain, closing my eyes for it
you clasped my hand

Across the barn the pritchel came down
like a hole punch
Blood sisters

IT COULD HAVE BEEN US

*Richard Benjamin Speck (December 6, 1941 – December 5, 1991) was
an American mass murderer who … tortured, raped, and murdered eight
student nurses from South Chicago Community Hospital on July 14, 1966.*

It was around my twelfth birthday
sunny and the days collapsed
like tempers
All our mothers wore pedal-pushers
slit to the knee
sleeveless blouses, bangles
My mother was a nurse
It could have been any one of us
she said. *It could have been me*
She rubbed goosebumps in summer

I paged obsessively through *Life* magazine
I couldn't stop imagining Cora
the nurse who got away
by hiding under a bed

At night, I checked our locks
front door, back, garbage shed
metal cool under my palms
Upstairs, my sister sweated and tossed
on July sheets
and I latched the windows tight so
no breeze could reach us

Night after night I flattened myself under my bed
as Cora had, crossed my arms
over my chest, heart pounding
listening for the sound of a man
pockmarked, greasy-haired, heavy-footed
in the hallway coming closer

Above me, the springs of my bed squeaked
I heard my mother climb
the stairs as if nothing was happening
as if the others before her
hadn't bloodily died
I heard the toilet flush, water run
her jewellery come off like bells
saw her naked ankles
move past

Home Birth

1)

The placenta is in a bowl
soaked with oils and
carrot blood, a bowl I use
for chopped vegetables

I want to plant it
fertilize azaleas or
peaches, but not out back of
the rental, so I freeze it

beside the poppyseed bread
and lentil casserole. Frozen
it is even more silvery and blue
Its veins delicate webs

and I imagine a heart
my own heart. The blood is
cracked like ice, dark red
congealed around the umbilicus

my husband cut
while most of it was still
inside me, after it stopped
pulsing. An inch thick

it felt like wet rubber
The placenta shimmered
radiant, meaty

pink and luminous
It took the shape
of the bowl perfectly
as if the bowl were my womb
My womb must have been

big enough to hold the bowl
then, before the baby came
though it's hard to imagine
comedic, an abracadabra of birth

2)

My mother-in-law is arriving
as she did with the last child
to look after me for a week
Back then she said

Let her cry
Crying develops babies' lungs
I sat in the living room
with a hot spot inside me

longing to answer my child
Give her half an hour, my
mother-in-law said
crocheting on the couch

Still, she is flying all this way
We buy groceries of the sort
a mother-in-law might like—
chickens and hams and lamb

Freezer full, we move the placenta
to the shelf beside the cheese and garlic
pods, cabbage and cauliflower
The baby is four days old

3)

My husband says I am not
to tell his mother I have
the placenta, it is a secret
It's not easy to hide

in the fridge or later in the car
on the way to the seaside market
I hold it between my feet
wrapped in a white plastic bag

Defrosted now
it splashes blood
on the underside of the bag—
Rorschach blots

My husband takes our
three-year-old and his mother
into the market
for kale and carrots

I should have
held out for a private beach
I am ashamed not to
have thought up some ceremony
of disposal instead of this
furtive dumping

as if the placenta were a corpse
from a murder

I descend a plank to the sea's edge
The ocean up close is not what I expected
the water murky, sloshing
a grey-tinged froth

polluted, cold green. A pop can
slaps the mooring
The baby's in a carrier on my chest
seven days old, asleep

I unwrap the placenta but
blood flies everywhere
smears my hands, my arms
my dress, my face

This, a week ago
was inside me
was part of me and the baby
I take a good long look

This one's for you, I tell my daughter
and I tilt the bowl
so the placenta
slides out, falls slowly

hits the sea, splashes
the umbilical cord
more buoyant
pulled under last

SONG OF THE SINGLE MOTHER

A mother alone dreams
fire above her bed

Every morning lights the wood stove
Every morning touches her daughters'
glassine shoulders and whispers
Little pumpkins, time to get up

Every morning takes a saucepan
from the belly of its mates and boils water
for porridge. Every morning combs snaggles
ties shoelaces, tugs leggings
pulls shirts over chests as thin
and bone-ribbed as leaky boats
Searches to find geography homework
makes lunches, strips sodden sheets
washes dishes, does laundry

Is impotent when a child is ill
chicken pox, influenza
ear infection
Carries limp girls to tepid
bathtubs, sponging and sponging to release
heat to skim away
from blistered cheeks
fever shadows on the wall

A mother alone is not innocent
Her shoulders round with burdens

Here is the weight of
oranges, potatoes, chicken
the price of groceries
Here is the weight of being
the only disciplinarian. Of worry
Dangers await her girls:
brain tumours, car accidents, cougars
A mother alone hopes over her children at night
Grow carefree and powerful
Grow sure of yourselves
A mother alone knows she is the safety
net into which they
must plunge—worries she isn't
strong enough, flexible enough
pleads never
to die and leave them

(Motherless
motherless babies)

Girls who appear, backpacks dragging
on the gravel driveway, hoofing it up the road
from the yellow bus
cranky, tired, concerned about
tests, boys, best friends, report cards, taunts
fighting endlessly over the remote
who gets a bigger piece of pie

A mother alone is helpless
with hopefulness
A mother alone is shredded
by love

too much too plentiful too lavish
cannot believe her own ferocity
Cannot respond other than to hug
and hush and pacify and say
Both, I love you both best

If the well goes dry, a mother alone
heats water in canning pots and pours it
boiling into the tub with an equal mix of cold
Dumps water over her child's head as
the girl howls and begs; massages in soap
A mother alone heats a towel
then lifts her daughter into
its warmth as if it were a womb

Leaves a nightlight pulsing on the wall

Understand, a mother alone can sing
but not hear
can walk upon the ground dragging her
footsteps behind her

Special Needs

When I gave her up to the attendant
at the airline she might have been
as small as she was inside me—
her lungs improperly formed, the spaces
between her fingers webbed, her skin
translucent and her beating heart visible
Special needs, I wanted to shout
and travel holding her like a wheelchair
or her hands upon me like crutches
But she was thirteen and capable, journeying to Florida
to visit her aunt and grandmother. It was hurricane
season. I imagined her listening to conchs
spreading her body hot as hibiscus
on the beaches. Yet when she called
it was to speak of Adam, her almost-cousin
my sister's foster son, all the things
gone wrong in his four years:
the father who'd snapped his baby sister
like red coral; the father who'd sodomized
him. That afternoon he'd swum with dolphins
my daughter said, and when he climbed from
the ocean he took her fingers, delicate as shells
thin as strands of seaweed, and urged her to slip them
inside him. My daughter wept
When my sister came on, she apologized, admitting
she was in over her head, that she'd held
her boy in the dolphin pen not knowing
if she could keep him, not knowing if
she could even love him

COLUMBINE

It was so hard to let her go off to high school
that spring. I wanted to take her wrist
and drag her with me instead

She made me drop her two blocks from school
Low on her hip she
flicked her fingers: *Go, go*

I don't have parents
I don't know you

It wasn't just Columbine
Children were dying gun deaths
all over the US
Teens were being snapped in two in car accidents
breakable as bread sticks
or taken to lonely woods
and crumpled like test papers

Later that summer at the swimming pool
teen boys tossed my daughter, their football
arms newly strong, voices
deep, sure, travelling out over the heads of toddlers
and kids in grade school
moms with infants

My daughter fought for footing on the bottom of the pool
came up sputtering
giggling
happy to be vanquished

THIS NEW COUNTRY

Green Attic

We buy a house, rub pigments to the walls
I am the first to think rose arbour, wisteria but
your hands hammer the form, dig the hole

We talk constantly about having
another child. The twin kittens
knock over flower pots, climb lace curtains
sharpen claws on our new sofa. The old cat
is crotchety, but you sit in the green attic
offering your lap, stroke her with comb
down to knots till she swipes
You measure your basal temperature, chart
fertile days. We rue impossibility
a child of our two bodies

It is the fifteenth of August
I never want this or the heat wave
to break

Soon the clouds will close up the sky
Outside the window the city trembles
soundlessly, fireworks rising like lightning

Tomorrow I will show you to everyone I love
and dream of marrying you

This New Country

We packed our bags and named
our destination: each other
climbed into the car
the bus, the plane
There would be no accidents
the airbag huddled under the dash
oxygen masks swarmed
above our heads, flotation devices
herded under our seats. I
couldn't stop looking at you. We
didn't know the new country even
four years later. I still don't know it
as you turn forty beside me
and flowers bloom. This country is
saturated with colour: azure
persimmon, indigo; with light:
dawn, the harsh light of noon, the washed
light of rain, dusk; with heat
We can't send postcards. We are dumb
exiled to grace

Dancing in the Kitchen 4 a.m.

I sizzle, hot along your arm
roll the sides of my shoes
hard heels blistering the floor
peppery, chipping sparks

                        You are swift boned
                                    brown eyed
against the static, the insistence of
hipbones, a rumba of fire

BLUE WOMEN

When you wanted to know
what I was thinking
I wasn't thinking
I was facing the mirror
lying against your right side
while beyond the window
the mountains rose like blue women

Seagulls tore the sky leaving squawks
I was looking at the shape of your
cheekbone, and at your
thin arm. Dusk, the smell of spring

We'd seen a dozen
hummingbirds in our garden
the hover of carmine throats. You
wrapped in a red towel. Me completely naked
It was Mother's Day; we had risen
and fallen as landscapes on the bed

I watched your breast which was fuller than
the night on my porch when I first undid
your buttons
It was almost our anniversary

Your nipple pointed down like a scolding
thumb, and I remembered how that first time
after you came, you prayed that
I would never leave you
and then I never left

Adoption

I watched you love the children
that first were mine and then became yours
Not an accident. Instead an accumulation:
storybooks, fights, reconciliations, laughter
The parent/child potato sack race, hopping
until you crossed the finish line and collapsed
into motherhood

WHAT WILL YOU DO WITH YOUR ONE WILD AND PRECIOUS LIFE?[3]

Today you tell me you'll be dead
in two years. There is bone pain:
lower back, shoulder and now rib
Your mother has just died
surprisingly after dental work
Your brother has lymphoma
I don't say the obvious: *Move sorrow*
out of your body
into your mind where you can conquer it
Honey, I say, *I'm here*

It's January but mild. The tree peony coils
leaf buds to its stem
Spring, that enemy of the depressed
is stalking our garden
with promises of life
Today you tell me you'll soon be dead
and I want to argue
What if spring fizzles, and summer thrums
and autumn creaks to winter
and spring renews
and you're still here
mowing the lawn

---

3   Mary Oliver, "The Summer Day."

THREAT

All summer I've been scanned
and prodded and tested for breast cancer
Three years ago it was you
this time it's me
The clinic inured to cold
the pink gown shed, my breast presented
X-rayed
twelve times
the room flushed with heat
windowless
a catheter up my milk duct

On our anniversary
we danced at Porteau Cove
in matching tuxedos
In the morning we cycled past
kayakers and cruise ships

The beauty of the summer rises in heat waves
In the yard the fountain burbles
our daughter fills our bedroom with
seven dozen balloons

Sex

Sometimes I mount you and fuck you and
you call out *fuck me* and I fuck you harder
palms spread wide on your ass
Other times we're workaday
intent just on coming
using vibrators for speed
Sometimes we watch porn
But sometimes all I want is your face
your lips, to run my tongue along the edge of your lashes
my fingertips to your cheeks, your nose, your chin

SCAR

I don't need light to find your scar
that rapturous score written across your chest
in treble clefs and half notes
I know where your flesh is seared
the surgeon pushed a hot brand into you

I know where she placed her scalpel
and cut you
while I sat in the waiting room
with worried families worrying

I could not have loved you more
than under the knife
calling to me from recovery
The surgeon might as well have cut me
without anesthetic

We pull fingertips across your numb skin
me, toting up losses
you, fascinated with where feeling begins

PARIS

Until the tiny shop in Montmartre, I believed we were
unbreachable—what day was that? Had we
gone to Les Puces de Saint-Ouen
or Giverny, or Musée d'Orsay? Had the
man with a butcher knife poised been taken
down by the storm of gendarmes?
I remember seeing water lilies everywhere
that day and the day after—it was Paris-Plage
along the urine-stinking banks of the Seine
there were jets and fountains of water clouding up in white mists
and L'Orangerie was still blue in my brain

But which day was it when I saw you beside the tiny shop?
We'd had coffee, I remember
in a low-ceilinged room full of received postcards
I saw you down the street looking at purses for our youngest
and felt a leap of happiness in my throat
as I always did when something you did said you loved our children

I didn't understand the possibility of endings then, I didn't know you
would soon say you weren't in love with me and had been hungering
to leave for thirteen years. What time of day was it? Just after noon
and we were off the Montmartre bus
I was taking atmospheric photographs
I ambled down the street to meet you, my grin large
I remember wanting to lift you in the street and swing you
until love made us soar

I came through the low door crouching to find you
shoving something quickly out of sight, your
eyes round with panic. I asked you to show me. You refused. I insisted
A gift for another woman. A small nothing, a vast something

We went shopping as if I hadn't noticed anything
Took the streetcar to Père Lachaise Cimetière, Gertrude's big grave
the afterthought of Alice

The knowledge of what I had almost not seen soaked through me
overnight as I lay in the shallow, chilly Parisian bathtub, the Seine
outside our window beyond the wavering draperies
What hotel was it? The sheets were voluptuous
as clean as we were suddenly dirty
your midsummer skin dark against them
At seven, I woke you and asked, and you said no
it was me, not her, not her, not her, who claimed your affections
she was someone inconsequential and confusing
You sweated as you spoke; your eyes darted sideways

That day, I moved along because moving along was what
my feet knew to do. It was my birthday, did I say?
We renewed our wedding vows, somehow—where was that?
Oh yes, of course. Under the Eiffel Tower, in a horse-drawn carriage
It was hot, it was July, it was Paris, it smelled of exhaustion
I forget what you said that day, except it was full of future
I remember the reassuring clop of the horse hooves as much
as I remember fingering old lace in Les Puces de Saint-Ouen
or Irving Penn's photographs in the Bresson Museum
as much as I remember the thousand red kisses on Oscar Wilde's grave

FLIGHT

Each bump along your bird's spine a worry bead, a
rosary under my fingertips
Begin by touch, you said
and I tried, I tried

Pigeons, blue glass, sailboat masts
ice, a thin stream of urban sound

Your bones were hollow, filled with air—
your keel, clavicles, skull
a complicated fretwork, an avian scaffolding
spliced with respiratory air sacs

You could fly
you could fly away from me
at any second
you could lift in an air current
and be gone

Begin by touch, you said
and reached for the scars
across my breasts
incised by scalpel
your wing tips brushing softly
bird prints on my skin

We lived where the gulls wheeled and swooped
Rainbow water taxies, dragon boaters
Kayakers on the creek
Begin by touch, you said
and I—
reached

but you were gone

Amalgam

Creatures must find each other for bodily comfort.

—Adrienne Rich

Sex is a language that stutters in your mouth lately
The love between us like your excised breast, gone and
remembered, made present by absence

Sex is a language I can still speak fluently, now that words have become
foes. I fear inarticulation; what is not said is always loud
I read between the parting of your lips where truth is a black hole

This stench, then, between us, do you smell it?
The rotting fruit in the green pail under the sink
the halitosis; the hot-flash sweat
the roses gone slimy in the garden

I have always been guileless around you
open—as if you had squatted in a harvest field and given birth
to me there, pushing
Because you *began* me in some essential way

Today I closed my office doors
and came to you naked and willing
my fingers warm and full of language
ready to translate and scribe my love

You were bicycling in bed, your perfect legs
scissoring the capsized dusk air
Outside it was cloudy, threatening rain. I got into bed
You turned toward me

Show me how you love me, I said

I needed tenderness
heat and exploration
but you, reluctant, distrustful
said, *Show* me *how you love* me

She Got the House

At last I knew it was over
She had not called or asked for anything
except to keep my mother's gifts
the furniture, the hammer, every bloom
in the garden, the cat, somehow my
decorating skill, my intellectual properties
She wanted no reconciliation

When we spoke, she said that she had
been waiting for me to die
for my heart to fail and give her
legitimate passage—

I drove across town fortified with nitroglycerin
and prayed for her to answer my knock
(on my own door)
begged on my blue-jeaned knees
Please, please, please
Give me back something from all I've lost

I was worsening in the way she'd hoped
Surgeries and hospitalizations

From behind the door, curtains parted
she stuck voodoo pins through my effigy
She whispered: *I will crush you*

She didn't understand she already had
The mouth I had sweetened to kiss
was black dust

Transplant

The surgeon snagged my heart
bleeding from its torn mouth
barbels antediluvian
held it up in the OR
pumping blood orgasms
atrium, tricuspid, ventricles, mitral valve

I didn't want to rip apart in doctors' hands
I wanted last words, rites, a significant
observation, acknowledgement
I wanted to say—something
Black commas twitched on my tongue
each one a scythe

Your obol, your exonumia on my tongue
five rivers of need
bleeding toward you
never arriving
Need, and need obliterated
and needed again
I was saved, or else I was dead
(or else I was dead)

HANDS

MANUS

I understand you by
touch not received
your hands from photographs

Your wrist, knuckles
the dorsal aspect
the soft finger pads of your palmar
your nails, their half moons, their scalloped tips
scaphoid, pisiform, capitate and hamate
phalanges, carpals, all your bones
tendons, muscles, nerves

The balletic bends
the flexion, the tridactyl configurations
all exposed in public
What a lesbian uses
she shows everyone
in the grocery store, at the library
fingering her sax

She tucks the world
into soft cradles of palm
into oblique arch She slides a hand
between her lover's legs and pauses—
cupping more continents
than this globe can hold
more firmaments of heat
volcanic and smouldering
than the earth's crust
more wet islands

(no woman is)
than the oceans

Synovial lining, muscle, ligament
tendon sheath, volar plate
and nerves
Your hands
turning over our future
before we've even met

WALKING IN THE FOREST

I wanted to tell you about the nurse tree
how she spit her young from the hips of her
stump to the sky, how, even so, I loved her
neighbour better, bark ripping into hidden crevices, moss
mounting her sides. I wanted to tell you

insertion, taking your hand, your wrist; I
swam dizzy all Sunday through kelp and
dulse, everything slurred around me
Understand I was touched
soft and far, lolling into what should

have frightened me, but did not
My mouth was sore and bruised. I smelled you
deep in my skin, a scorch
You appeared before me
like linked scarves out of someone's sleeve
like those trees—significant, utterly simple

VIOLIN

Today at slow-flowing Verde River
a woman fished for bass. I thought of
Nile crocodiles and a woman whose right breast
was snatched away on the banks of the Kunene River
in the desert, in the mountains
I thought of that woman who belonged to her
man's harem, and I thought about
the children tending goats, about
the Goliath heron swooping above our skiff
its lurid racketing wingspan. Above this green river
red-tailed hawks circled, riding the air currents
wing feathers flicked upwards
The turquoise of your shirt matched my
new ring exactly. Understand me:
when you stripped, a yellow oriole
darted past, as on the Kunene yellow weavers flitted
through reeds. Your bra, your shorts, your underwear
fell to a rock. You stood in the red mud
naked, your skin freckled and burned
your hair wild with curls. I made your
photograph as you waded deep, the curve of your
back the shape of a violin

Sedona, Arizona

I heard the nuns conversing in German
white habits and swinging crosses, they
climbed the red rocks, hands sizzling
I imagined their lives at night
in oppressive Phoenix heat
sweat blooming between breasts
ashen bloodless thighs
(the shock of springy hair, moist petals)
women in dark solitudes
rubbing hard beads

At the Frank Lloyd Wright church
candles flickered behind red vases hot with wishes
Please make Richard concede and sign all the papers
Please sell my house in AZ

You on the rocks getting farther away
untouchable
(loneliness is part of this story)
The outcroppings in the rocks you clung to were not even
as large as your nail beds
Contrails shredded clouds
A vortex juniper spiraled above me
You spidered too small to see
I heard you shout my name from the apex of Bell Rock

At the church, a woman curled her hand around a red vase
light through fingers
the way, at moments, women in love go transparent

Harsh sun on my skin
Rosaries swaying like clocks
In the churchyard, I put my hand through Jesus' ribs
The body could refuse refuge, the body could refuse
time and lethargy. The body could refuse
anything that binds it to earth

ECLOSURE

i.

Her palm is a cocoon, a tuck and roll of gold fibres, a mummification, an artful cigar. *Join this metamorphosis*, she says. She is an extreme athlete. I am—something else. Like other women clinging to the rock face, her hands shaped into claws, she says, *I will not be broken*. Like other women cycling exhausted and blue, her hands shaped into pincers, she says, *I will not yield*. The cocoon dangles between her fingers like a cashew, a curled cylindrical heart, but it isn't just a heart, I understand that, I understand partiality and totality. I know what she is offering

ii.

This hand of hers, this strong hand of hers, all of this hand, fingernails, knuckles, small hairs, bones, tendons, veins, hangnails, skin, cuticles, opposable thumb, all that it has held or reached for or touched or felt— *freezing, a burn*—has been inside me, on the fulcrum of its flexible wrist, caught within me as if the vault of my vagina were a prison with pulsing maroon bars from which she could not escape until she promised me something deeper than blood. I saw orange and I saw green, an aurora borealis of the bedroom, and when I closed my eyes there were explosions of light, sparklers in black skies. When she pulled out, it felt like I was giving birth

iii.

A cocoon is papery, silken, spun. It waits for the yellow juice of spring, tucked red and vulval inside, its miniature heart beating, beating. It is fortitude and promise and patience. It is dry shelter, infinitesimal hungers that slowly unfurl into untenable wholes

iv.

How do I explain to her? I am pinioned by loss. I am stapled to the examining table of my past

v.

Lines waterfall down her fingers where I have run my damp tongue. Her finger of Saturn. Her finger of Apollo. Her finger of Jupiter. The gods, the planets around which I have climaxed. I held this hand, dripping and curled and warm, just after it emerged. I kissed it as if it were an infant I needed to stir to life, as if it would hold to my breasts to suckle, as if in its stunned placid present it would pull from me nourishment. As if I could guide its future. As if I could keep it away from the glacial waters, the avalanche, the barreling car

vi.

I look away from the cocoon into her eyes. I look into cornea, into sclera, into iris and pupil. Things that are blue: skies, blueberries, violets, bluebonnets, jays, bluebirds, turquoise, sapphires, fish, ocean. Ice. In her eyes chips of Antarctica float

vii.

Her hand still hovers steady as a midge, an invitation, the cocoon elliptical and swinging, no longer sessile, waggling now, the cocoon like a miniature wasp's nest with preposterous contracts, wings and flight and beauty, hidden inside. Jailbreak begins

viii.

I am too hungry. I am too huge. I am too slow. It is too late for me

ix.

She says, *I am the scent of hyacinths. I am the smell of blue.* I say, *I am scared.* She says, *Risk.* I take her hand. I take her hand which has known all the chambers of me, all my red, pulsing secrets, all my lost rooms. *Come outside,* she says

x.

I do

Birding in Central Park

We are twenty-five birders wearing binoculars in harnesses:
Fujinon, Fraser Optics
Lenore, our guide, speaks of irruptive species
We've covered the three introduced birds
rock pigeon, starlings, finches
(three introduced feelings that fall implores:
wistfulness, sorrow, comfort)
Lenore says, *There's a red-bellied woodpecker*
There's a junco on the London plane tree
on the right where the branch hangs down
See it moving?

We pass the Loch, the Children's Glade
Runner! Lenore cries and we disperse flocklike from the path
a jogger thumps by in Spandex
We move as one geeky muscle
pulling each other along like hamstrings
One woman asks another
for the health of her grandchildren
Her unhappy boy has braces
Did your husband get the colonoscopy?
another woman says

We've had arboreal birds, Lenore says
peckers, probers and creepers
branch tip gleaners

Now we head up to the top of the Great Hill
climb beside elm
and sumacs lit with fire

There's a male yellow-bellied sapsucker halfway up that trunk
and there, a palm warbler

Hey, look, I say, *is that a tufted titmouse*
That branch, close to the water?

Lenore says, *Try not to point*

LAUNDRY, LONG DISTANCE

For eight weeks we writhed in the sheets
then kissed goodbye

After you left, I laundered your clothing
carried your clean hot shirts to my bed
the tender smell of fabric softener
and I picked up a grey t-shirt, and began
(as women have always begun) to fold it
turning your shirt right-side out, my hands in the collar, shaking it
digging for sleeves, lifting it
(as if it were you, as if it still contained your hard shoulders, your
round breasts) my hands along the top seams
giving a shake before folding it over, blade to blade
turning in the arms, doubling it over, laying it down

The column of shirts, when I stacked them on the shelf
was muted: sage green, off-white, faded maroon
like the ordinary, unremarkable way I had begun to love you

HURRICANE IN NEW YORK

This morning as winds rip open
our windows
like silent hands under
our sheets
the walls of your cunt
oscillate, pumping
throats of multiple bullfrogs
and I want you, I want you

This part of your body
is music riffing to wind
sultry, wild, dirty
musky, heady, sharp
The fifth flavour, umami
coats my tongue

Below our loft
red lights glow on Amsterdam
the carless streets grey and wet
placards tarps plastic bags fly:
Flu Shots Today flaps against scaffolding
umbrella whips down 86th
On 57th, a crane collapses
substation on 14th fails
green and flashing
Wall Street floods

This part of your body
slams against my fingers as
waves hurl ashore in Battery Park

SLEEPLESS

We did not sleep and were made insane by it, and loved the stupidity
Gads, it was just the thing, all that rutting, our senses electrified
honeyed bee stings, slow-sinking mudslicks—sex
meted out in silken slaps on a slow summer landscape of skin
most extraordinary, more to us than Lamborghinis
or Ecosse cycles, more than soaring through cerulean skies, skin was
licked, bitten, scorched, twisted, puckered, rubbed raw, hickeyed
blown on, finger-tipped, heated, cooled, exalted—

every time we fucked it was brand new, *brand new*, I say
like a cotyledon leaf through spring soil, like starlight brimming night
every time we fucked it was groundbreaking, her voice rising
in mewls and murmurs and mine a hosanna, a liturgical worship—
did we hear a choir of lesbians? cries and exclamations and groans
and caught breath and occasional exhortations as leg cramps or
ovaries knocked or a nipple tweaked past good pain—

let me talk about her frankness, the way she opened me as an orange
stripping off bumpy rind, the way she peeled me so I came apart
in sections juicy and dripping through her hands
my head thrown back
my throat rippling, how she asked me to show her
fucking myself ... I stopped time
for that, wouldn't you? *Fuck*, wouldn't you?
masturbating naked on her deck in the sunshine
my skin hot and prickling ... if you could, wouldn't you
stop everything and just—

and the first thing, no, it wasn't the first thing
but neither of us was keeping notes ... the actual first thing

was the moon fingering shadows through arbutus leaves
while she lifted her Folk Fest t-shirt
and I moved like silk behind her, my breasts globular and firm
and ran my tongue up the bones of her spine, bump, valley
bump, valley and so on, before a kiss, I mean, I seriously mean that—
before a kiss, or even, the next night in another town
weeping against her, sobbing for the cruelties of illness—her fist
struggled to fit inside me, slow lubed penetration, agonizingly sweet
and harsh, my cunt became a balloon, a hollow, filling
with this woman's richest tactility, and began to—

she began interphalangeal articulations, I mean she began to move
against me, my red leaking bruised flesh
a postural rotation, I mean her wrist turned
and I reached to feel her there
fisting me, and I could see her move inside me by watching above
my pelvic bone, the shape of her fingers almost visible
and I was gobsmacked that a woman
was taking me like that, punching me, if you will, if you go where
bdsm goes (which we didn't—we did not, that, quite)
I arched my back, began to ululate
and roll my eyes back as she flung me
over Saturn like an extra moon, like Titan. I was all head and no head
at the same time, blown like a gunshot, blown into space—

eventually everything ends, and when she slipped out
it felt endless and hard-edged and astonishing and I melted
and held her hand, and it was soft and humid
I thought how it was, touching her wrist
while it was inside me, I marvelled at that—
we were doing everything—it's not like it stopped there
 I mean, would you?—

hot air huffed into our earlobes, kisses, teeth nipping
we moved our vulvas together, rubbing them fast like itches
laughing and turning over and over like rolling softballs
and what I call Exorcist Sex
where I struggled back to reality and my head
was on backwards—

wait, pause here, that's barely the start, barely registers what it was like
on the couch, on the floor, on the beach, on the deck, in the lake
with the dive-bombing dragonflies and the lily pads and the reeds
all day, no matter where I went, the bank, the beach
I saw her ass, her cunt, her clit, her rough nipples
her kneeling above me, her fingers moving in her own black bush
her palm moving up her ribs to cradle her breast
her fingers touching her own nipple—

it was colour, I kept seeing her in blues and I painted her like that
I saw her in an explosion of oranges and reds and I painted
that too, I kept hearing her as cello music and I painted
that too, I thought of the things that were stop-frame—
I sucked my own nipple, I sucked her cock, her tongue
was everything an artist could pray for—articulate—

we went to films until our eyes bled and while I watched
I thought of the rounds of her tits moving over the twin globes
of my ass, I thought of the night we fucked under a meteor shower
stars exploding over her head, but also I spent a lot of time
inside her, and the moment when I slipped in her drip
when I entered her elastic vagina, I always gave a gasp
a cry of devotion and then her sympathetic and parasympathetic
nerves either gripped me or belled around me
her vagina a spongy muscle that sucked at me

and I lowered my face to her cunt
that valley between muscular thighs
the sharp, musky white-peach taste
that salty, tangy, lemony, acidic flesh over hard bone, the sloppy sound
of kisses, and unhooding her clit and finding that smooth bead
and sucking it, jittering the flit of her clit—but, but—everything
fuck—

everything we did soaked into my skin and heart like bleach
down through the layers of my epidermis to mark me
alter me. We didn't sleep and were made crazy
by it, lunatical, fresh—every day was stupidly sunny
and even as summer passed and fall began
it would not rain

THE LOVERS I HAVE LOVED

Whatever happened
I loved them by instinct
and came to them shedding my skin
in the remarkable length of summer
in the blue northern seas
in the pattern of the arbutus on the deck
in the red hills
on the crowded streets of Shanghai
in Central Park
in Californian art galleries
Whatever happened—
the days grew short and the sun
broke against skyscrapers
and the nights froze beyond all comfort—

Whatever happened to us
after they'd loved me by instinct
and had come to me shedding trepidation
in the hush of slow, interior movements
in the stillness of heat
in the white swell of the harvest moon
Whatever happened
after the fawn stood on its hind hooves
after the elephant seals molted
after the birds migrated

Whatever happened
(we did not tarry, we did not root)
I still walk toward them
and lay my palm upon each cheek
a lover's palm on lovers' cheeks

ACKNOWLEDGEMENTS

HUGE THANKS to my editor, Patricia Young, a stalwart and engaged champion to these works who cultivated the shapeless forest until it became a tended garden, and to the Caitlin Press team for bringing this book to fruition. I am grateful to the Canada Council for the Arts and the BC Arts Council for substantial support over the years, and to the Banff Centre for the Arts, where some of these poems were first conceived.

I am lucky to have had a number of patient ears listen to versions of these works, in particular Bon Fabian, Anjuli Pandavar, Julia Balén, Luna Nordin and Dimitra Douskos. I am grateful to Julian Thorsteinson for letting me stay in her place in Paris, and Susan MacRae for her generous help. Without Sandy Shreve, an extraordinary support, and Kate Braid, this book would not have found its current home. Thanks to Cornelia Hoogland for continually backing my efforts. Thank you also to the poets of the Electronic Garret, especially Tanis MacDonald, Maureen Hynes, Shannon Maguire, Arleen Paré and Yvonne Blomer; your work and wisdom found its way to me at pivotal moments.

I am grateful to my children, Sarah Hamilton and Meghann Hamilton-Ritson, for their dependable, beautiful love.

NOTES

"Love will burst into a thousand shapes" is a quote from a letter by Frida Kahlo.

"Home Birth" first appeared in the *Malahat Review* no. 99, summer 1992.

The poem sequence called "Special Needs" was one of five winners in the *Prairie Fire* "The Long and the Short of It" contest and appeared in volume 15, no. 4, winter 1994–95.

"Our Terrible Good Luck" first appeared as "The Sick Boy" in *Poetry Canada Review* 15, no. 1.

"The Small White Heel, " now called "It Could Have Been Us," appeared at arcpoetry.ca in March, 2012.

"Sleepless" appeared in different form in *Numéro Cinq* in January, 2013.

"Lesbian Sex" was a finalist for the Montreal Prize 2013.

"A Terrible Lucidity, 1890: Vincent Van Gogh," "The Lucite Box: Edward Degas," and "Woman with a Mango by Gauguin: Etta Cone" appeared in *Canadian Poetries*, 2014.

"War Photograph" appeared in *Shout Out UK*, 2014.

"Eclosure" first appeared in *Plenitude Magazine,* Issue 4.

PHOTO SHAWNA FLETCHER

JANE EATON HAMILTON is the author of eight books, including two volumes of poetry and two of short fiction. Her books have been included in the *Guardian's* Best of the Year list and have been shortlisted for several awards, including the Mind Book Award, the Ferro-Grumley Award, the Vancity Book Prize, the Pat Lowther Award, and the BC Book Prizes, as well as being on the *Sunday Times* bestsellers list. Her chapbook, *Going Santa Fe*, won the League of Canadian Poets Chapbook Award. Her short work, which has appeared in such publications as the *New York Times, Seventeen* magazine, *Macleans,* the *Globe and Mail, Salon,* the *Missouri Review* and *Numéro Cinq*, has won many prizes including, twice, first prize for fiction in the CBC Literary Prizes and Canada Writes competition, in 2003 and 2014 respectively.

Jane is also a photographer and visual artist. She was one of the litigants in Canada's same-sex marriage case. She lives in Vancouver. More can be found at janeeatonhamilton.wordpress.com.